This Journal Belongs To:

COPYRIGHT©
ALL RIGHTS RESERVED. THIS BOOK OR ANY PORTION
THEREOF MAY NOT BE REPRODUCED OR USED IN ANY
MANNER WHATSOEVER WITHOUT THE EXPRESS WRITTEN
PERMISSION OF THE AUTHOR.

A

Date: _____
Suppliers: _____
Project: _____

Wax and Wick Used.

Costs.

Fragrance Used, % Used, Pour Temperature.

Wax Melt Top Temperature and Pour Temperature.

Dye Used, % Used and Temperature Added.

Cure Time.

Notes:

Pass or Fail? _____

Candle Jar Used.

A

Date: _____
Suppliers: _____
Project: _____

Wax and Wick Used.

Costs.

Fragrance Used, % Used. Pour Temperature.

Wax Melt Top Temperature and Pour Temperature.

Dye Used, % Used and Temperature Added.

Cure Time.

Notes:

Pass or Fail? _____

Candle Jar Used.

A

Date: _____
Suppliers: _____
Project: _____

Wax and Wick Used.

Costs.

Fragrance Used, % Used, Pour Temperature.

Wax Melt Top Temperature and Pour Temperature.

Dye Used, % Used and Temperature Added.

Cure Time.

Notes:

Pass or Fail? _____

Candle Jar Used.

A

Date: _____
Suppliers: _____
Project: _____

Wax and Wick Used.

Costs.

Fragrance Used, % Used, Pour Temperature.

Wax Melt Top Temperature and Pour Temperature.

Dye Used, % Used and Temperature Added.

Cure Time.

Notes:

Pass or Fail? _____

Candle Jar Used.

B

Date : _____
Suppliers : _____
Project : _____

Wax and Wick Used

Costs

Fragrance Used, % Used, Pour Temperature.

Wax Melt Top Temperature and Pour Temperature.

Dye Used, % Used and Temperature Added

Cure Time:

Notes:

Pass or Fail ? _____

Candle Jar Used

B

Date: _____
Suppliers: _____
Project: _____

Wax and Wick Used

Costs

Fragrance Used, % Used. Pour Temperature.

Wax Melt Top Temperature and Pour Temperature.

Dye Used, % Used and Temperature Added

Cure Time:

Notes:

Pass or Fail? _____

Candle Jar Used

B

Date: _____
Suppliers: _____
Project: _____

Wax and Wick Used

Costs

Fragrance Used, % Used, Pour Temperature.

Wax Melt Top Temperature and Pour Temperature. _____

Dye Used, % Used and Temperature Added

Cure Time:

Notes:

Pass or Fail? _____

Candle Jar Used

B

Date: _____
Suppliers: _____
Project: _____

Wax and Wick Used

Costs

Fragrance Used, % Used, Pour Temperature.

Wax Melt Top Temperature and Pour Temperature.

Dye Used, % Used and Temperature Added

Cure Time:

Notes:

Pass or Fail? _____

Candle Jar Used

C

Date: _____
Suppliers: _____
Project: _____

Wax and Wick Used.

Costs.

Fragrance Used, % Used. Pour Temperature.

Wax Melt Top Temperature and Pour Temperature.

Dye Used, % Used and Temperature Added.

Cure Time.

Notes:

Pass or Fail? _____

Candle Jar Used.

C

Date: _____
Suppliers: _____
Project: _____

Wax and Wick Used.

Costs.

Fragrance Used, % Used, Pour Temperature.

Wax Melt Top Temperature and Pour Temperature.

Dye Used, % Used and Temperature Added.

Cure Time.

Notes:

Pass or Fail? _____

Candle Jar Used.

C

Date: _____
Suppliers: _____
Project: _____

Wax and Wick Used.

Costs.

Fragrance Used, % Used, Pour Temperature.

Wax Melt Top Temperature and Pour Temperature.

Dye Used, % Used and Temperature Added.

Cure Time.

Notes:

Pass or Fail? _____

Candle Jar Used.

C

Date: _____
Suppliers: _____
Project: _____

Wax and Wick Used.

Costs.

Fragrance Used, % Used, Pour Temperature.

Wax Melt Top Temperature and Pour Temperature. _____

Dye Used, % Used and Temperature Added.

Cure Time.

Notes:

Pass or Fail? _____

Candle Jar Used.

D

Date: _____
Suppliers: _____
Project: _____

Wax and Wick Used.

Costs.

Fragrance Used, % Used, Pour Temperature.

Wax Melt Top Temperature and Pour Temperature.

Dye Used, % Used and Temperature Added.

Cure Time.

Notes:

Pass or Fail? _____

Candle Jar Used.

D

Date: _____
Suppliers: _____
Project: _____

Wax and Wick Used.

Costs.

Fragrance Used, % Used, Pour Temperature.

Wax Melt Top Temperature and Pour Temperature.

Dye Used, % Used and Temperature Added.

Cure Time.

Notes:

Pass or Fail? _____

Candle Jar Used.

D

Date: _____
Suppliers: _____
Project: _____

Wax and Wick Used.

Costs.

Fragrance Used, % Used, Pour Temperature.

Wax Melt Top Temperature and Pour Temperature.

Dye Used, % Used and Temperature Added.

Cure Time.

Notes:

Pass or Fail? _____

Candle Jar Used.

D

Date: _____
Suppliers: _____
Project: _____

Wax and Wick Used.

Costs.

Fragrance Used.
% Used. Pour Temperature.

Wax Melt Top Temperature and Pour Temperature.

Dye Used.
% Used and Temperature Added.

Cure Time.

Notes:

Pass or Fail? _____

Candle Jar Used.

E

Date: _____
Suppliers: _____
Project: _____

Wax and Wick Used.

Costs.

Fragrance Used, % Used, Pour Temperature.

Wax Melt Top Temperature and Pour Temperature.

Dye Used, % Used and Temperature Added.

Cure Time.

Notes:

Pass or Fail? _____

Candle Jar Used.

E

Date :

Suppliers :

Project :

Wax and Wick Used.

Costs.

Fragrance Used, % Used. Pour Temperature.

Wax Melt Top Temperature and Pour Temperature.

Dye Used, % Used and Temperature Added.

Cure Time.

Notes:

Pass or Fail ?

Candle Jar Used.

E

Date: _____
Suppliers: _____
Project: _____

Wax and Wick Used.

Costs.

Fragrance Used, % Used, Pour Temperature.

Wax Melt Top Temperature and Pour Temperature.

Dye Used, % Used and Temperature Added.

Cure Time.

Notes:

Pass or Fail? _____

Candle Jar Used.

E

Date : _____
Suppliers : _____
Project : _____

Wax and Wick Used.

Costs.

Fragrance Used, % Used, Pour Temperature.

Wax Melt Top Temperature and Pour Temperature.

Dye Used, % Used and Temperature Added.

Cure Time.

Notes:

Pass or Fail ? _____

Candle Jar Used.

F

Date:
Suppliers:
Project:

Wax and Wick Used.

Costs.

Fragrance Used, % Used, Pour Temperature.

Wax Melt Top Temperature and Pour Temperature.

Dye Used, % Used and Temperature Added.

Cure Time.

Notes:

Pass or Fail ?

Candle Jar Used.

F

Date : _____
Suppliers : _____
Project : _____

Wax and Wick Used.

Costs.

Fragrance Used, % Used, Pour Temperature.

Wax Melt Top Temperature and Pour Temperature.

Dye Used, % Used and Temperature Added.

Cure Time.

Notes:

Pass or Fail ? _____

Candle Jar Used.

F

Date : _____

Suppliers : _____

Project : _____

Wax and Wick Used.

Costs.

Fragrance Used, % Used, Pour Temperature.

Wax Melt Top Temperature and Pour Temperature.

Dye Used, % Used and Temperature Added.

Cure Time.

Notes:

Pass or Fail ? _____

Candle Jar Used.

F

Date: _____
Suppliers: _____
Project: _____

Wax and Wick Used.

Costs.

Fragrance Used, % Used. Pour Temperature.

Wax Melt Top Temperature and Pour Temperature.

_____

Dye Used, % Used and Temperature Added.

Cure Time.

Notes:

Pass or Fail? _____

Candle Jar Used.

G

Date:
Suppliers:
Project:

Wax and Wick Used.

Costs.

Fragrance Used, % Used, Pour Temperature.

Wax Melt Top Temperature and Pour Temperature.

Dye Used, % Used and Temperature Added.

Cure Time.

Notes:

Pass or Fail?

Candle Jar Used.

G

Date : _____
Suppliers : _____
Project : _____

Wax and Wick Used.

Costs.

Fragrance Used, % Used, Pour Temperature.

Wax Melt Top Temperature and Pour Temperature. _____

Dye Used, % Used and Temperature Added.

Cure Time.

Notes:

Pass or Fail ? _____

Candle Jar Used.

G

Date: _____
Suppliers: _____
Project: _____

Wax and Wick Used.

Costs.

Fragrance Used, % Used, Pour Temperature.

Wax Melt Top Temperature and Pour Temperature.

Dye Used, % Used and Temperature Added.

Cure Time.

Notes:

Pass or Fail? _____

Candle Jar Used.

G

Date: _____

Suppliers: _____

Project: _____

Wax and Wick Used.

Costs.

Fragrance Used, % Used, Pour Temperature.

Wax Melt Top Temperature and Pour Temperature.

Dye Used, % Used and Temperature Added.

Cure Time.

Notes:

Pass or Fail? _____

Candle Jar Used.

H

Date: _____
Suppliers: _____
Project: _____

Wax and Wick Used.

Costs.

Fragrance Used, % Used, Pour Temperature.

Wax Melt Top Temperature and Pour Temperature.

Dye Used, % Used and Temperature Added.

Cure Time.

Notes:

Pass or Fail? _____

Candle Jar Used.

H

Date: _____
Suppliers: _____
Project: _____

Wax and Wick Used.

Costs.

Fragrance Used, % Used, Pour Temperature.

Wax Melt Top Temperature and Pour Temperature. _____

Dye Used, % Used and Temperature Added.

Cure Time.

Notes:

Pass or Fail? _____

Candle Jar Used.

H

Date: ....
Suppliers: ....
Project: ....

Wax and Wick Used.

Costs.

Fragrance Used, % Used, Pour Temperature.

Wax Melt Top Temperature and Pour Temperature.

Dye Used, % Used and Temperature Added.

Cure Time.

Notes:

Pass or Fail? ....

Candle Jar Used.

H

Date: _____
Suppliers: _____
Project: _____

Wax and Wick Used.

Costs.

Fragrance Used, % Used, Pour Temperature.

Wax Melt Top Temperature and Pour Temperature.

Dye Used, % Used and Temperature Added.

Cure Time.

Notes:

Pass or Fail? _____

Candle Jar Used.

I

Date: _____
Suppliers: _____
Project: _____

Wax and Wick Used.

Costs.

Fragrance Used, % Used. Pour Temperature.

Wax Melt Top Temperature and Pour Temperature.

Dye Used, % Used and Temperature Added.

Cure Time.

Notes:

Pass or Fail? _____

Candle Jar Used.

I

Date: _____
Suppliers: _____
Project: _____

Wax and Wick Used.

Costs.

Fragrance Used, % Used. Pour Temperature.

Wax Melt Top Temperature and Pour Temperature.

Dye Used, % Used and Temperature Added.

Cure Time.

Notes:

Pass or Fail? _____

Candle Jar Used.

I

Date: _____
Suppliers: _____
Project: _____

Wax and Wick Used.

Costs.

Fragrance Used, % Used, Pour Temperature.

Wax Melt Top Temperature and Pour Temperature.

Dye Used, % Used and Temperature Added.

Cure Time.

Notes:

Pass or Fail? _____

Candle Jar Used.

I

Date: _____
Suppliers: _____
Project: _____

Wax and Wick Used.

Costs.

Fragrance Used, % Used, Pour Temperature.

Wax Melt Top Temperature and Pour Temperature. _____

Dye Used, % Used and Temperature Added.

Cure Time.

Notes:

Pass or Fail? _____

Candle Jar Used.

J

Date : ....
Suppliers : ....
Project : ....

Wax and Wick Used.

Costs.

Fragrance Used, % Used, Pour Temperature.

Wax Melt Top Temperature and Pour Temperature.

Dye Used, % Used and Temperature Added.

Cure Time.

Notes:

Pass or Fail ? ....

Candle Jar Used.

J

Date: _____
Suppliers: _____
Project: _____

Wax and Wick Used.

Costs.

Fragrance Used, % Used, Pour Temperature.

Wax Melt Top Temperature and Pour Temperature.

Dye Used, % Used and Temperature Added.

Cure Time.

Notes:

Pass or Fail? _____

Candle Jar Used.

J

Date : _____
Suppliers : _____
Project : _____

Wax and Wick Used.

Costs.

Fragrance Used, % Used, Pour Temperature.

Wax Melt Top Temperature and Pour Temperature.

Dye Used, % Used and Temperature Added.

Cure Time.

Notes:

Pass or Fail ? _____

Candle Jar Used.

J

Date: ....
Suppliers: ....
Project: ....

Wax and Wick Used.

Costs.

Fragrance Used, % Used. Pour Temperature.

Wax Melt Top Temperature and Pour Temperature.

Dye Used, % Used and Temperature Added.

Cure Time.

Notes:

Pass or Fail? ....

Candle Jar Used.

Date: _____
Suppliers: _____
Project: _____

Wax and Wick Used.

Costs.

Fragrance Used. % Used. Pour Temperature.

Wax Melt Top Temperature and Pour Temperature.

Dye Used. % Used and Temperature Added.

Cure Time.

Notes:

Pass or Fail? _____

Candle Jar Used.

K

Date : _____
Suppliers : _____
Project : _____

Wax and Wick Used.

Costs.

Fragrance Used, % Used, Pour Temperature.

Wax Melt Top Temperature and Pour Temperature. _____

Dye Used, % Used and Temperature Added.

Cure Time.

Notes:

Pass or Fail ? _____

Candle Jar Used.

Date: _____
Suppliers: _____
Project: _____

Wax and Wick Used.

Costs.

Fragrance Used, % Used. Pour Temperature.

Wax Melt Top Temperature and Pour Temperature.

Dye Used, % Used and Temperature Added.

Cure Time.

Notes:

Pass or Fail? _____

Candle Jar Used.

Date : _____
Suppliers : _____
Project : _____

Wax and Wick Used.

Costs.

Fragrance Used, % Used, Pour Temperature.

Wax Melt Top Temperature and Pour Temperature.

Dye Used, % Used and Temperature Added.

Cure Time.

Notes:

Pass or Fail ? _____

Candle Jar Used.

L

Date: _____
Suppliers: _____
Project: _____

Wax and Wick Used.

Costs.

Fragrance Used, % Used. Pour Temperature.

Wax Melt Top Temperature and Pour Temperature.

Dye Used, % Used and Temperature Added.

Cure Time.

Notes:

Pass or Fail? _____

Candle Jar Used.

L

Date: _____
Suppliers: _____
Project: _____

Wax and Wick Used.

Costs.

Fragrance Used, % Used, Pour Temperature.

Wax Melt Top Temperature and Pour Temperature.

Dye Used, % Used and Temperature Added.

Cure Time.

Notes:

Pass or Fail? _____

Candle Jar Used.

L

Date: _____
Suppliers: _____
Project: _____

Wax and Wick Used.

Costs.

Fragrance Used, % Used. Pour Temperature.

Wax Melt Top Temperature and Pour Temperature.

Dye Used, % Used and Temperature Added.

Cure Time.

Notes:

Pass or Fail? _____

Candle Jar Used.

L

Date : _____
Suppliers : _____
Project : _____

Wax and Wick Used.

Costs.

Fragrance Used, % Used, Pour Temperature.

Wax Melt Top Temperature and Pour Temperature.

Dye Used, % Used and Temperature Added.

Cure Time.

Notes:

Pass or Fail ? _____

Candle Jar Used.

M

Date: _____
Suppliers: _____
Project: _____

Wax and Wick Used.

Costs.

Fragrance Used, % Used, Pour Temperature.

Wax Melt Top Temperature and Pour Temperature.

Dye Used, % Used and Temperature Added.

Cure Time.

Notes:

Pass or Fail? _____

Candle Jar Used.

M

Date: _____
Suppliers: _____
Project: _____

Wax and Wick Used.

Costs.

Fragrance Used, % Used. Pour Temperature.

Wax Melt Top Temperature and Pour Temperature.

Dye Used, % Used and Temperature Added.

Cure Time.

Notes:

Pass or Fail? _____

Candle Jar Used.

M

Date: _____
Suppliers: _____
Project: _____

Wax and Wick Used.

Costs.

Fragrance Used, % Used, Pour Temperature.

Wax Melt Top Temperature and Pour Temperature.

Dye Used, % Used and Temperature Added.

Cure Time.

Notes:

Pass or Fail? _____

Candle Jar Used.

M

Date: _____
Suppliers: _____
Project: _____

Wax and Wick Used.

Costs.

Fragrance Used, % Used, Pour Temperature.

Wax Melt Top Temperature and Pour Temperature.

Dye Used, % Used and Temperature Added.

Cure Time.

Notes:

Pass or Fail? _____

Candle Jar Used.

n

Date: _____
Suppliers: _____
Project: _____

Wax and Wick Used.

Costs.

Fragrance Used, % Used, Pour Temperature.

Wax Melt Top Temperature and Pour Temperature.

Dye Used, % Used and Temperature Added.

Cure Time.

Notes:

Pass or Fail? _____

Candle Jar Used.

n

Date : _____

Suppliers : _____

Project : _____

Wax and Wick Used.

Costs.

Fragrance Used, % Used, Pour Temperature.

Wax Melt Top Temperature and Pour Temperature.

Dye Used, % Used and Temperature Added.

Cure Time.

Notes:

Pass or Fail ? _____

Candle Jar Used.

n

Date: _____
Suppliers: _____
Project: _____

Wax and Wick Used.

Costs.

Fragrance Used, % Used, Pour Temperature.

Wax Melt Top Temperature and Pour Temperature.

Dye Used, % Used and Temperature Added.

Cure Time.

Notes:

Pass or Fail? _____

Candle Jar Used.

n

Date: _____
Suppliers: _____
Project: _____

Wax and Wick Used.

Costs.

Fragrance Used, % Used, Pour Temperature.

Wax Melt Top Temperature and Pour Temperature.

Dye Used, % Used and Temperature Added.

Cure Time.

Notes:

Pass or Fail? _____

Candle Jar Used.

0

Date : _____
Suppliers : _____
Project : _____

Wax and Wick Used.

Costs.

Fragrance Used, % Used, Pour Temperature.

Wax Melt Top Temperature and Pour Temperature.

Dye Used, % Used and Temperature Added.

Cure Time.

Notes:

Pass or Fail ? _____

Candle Jar Used.

0

Date: _____
Suppliers: _____
Project: _____

Wax and Wick Used.

Costs.

Fragrance Used, % Used, Pour Temperature.

Wax Melt Top Temperature and Pour Temperature.

Dye Used, % Used and Temperature Added.

Cure Time.

Notes:

Pass or Fail? _____

Candle Jar Used.

Date:
Suppliers:
Project:

Wax and Wick Used.

Costs.

Fragrance Used, % Used, Pour Temperature.

Wax Melt Top Temperature and Pour Temperature.

Dye Used, % Used and Temperature Added.

Cure Time.

Notes:

Pass or Fail?

Candle Jar Used.

Date: _____
Suppliers: _____
Project: _____

Wax and Wick Used.

Costs.

Fragrance Used, % Used, Pour Temperature.

Wax Melt Top Temperature and Pour Temperature.

Dye Used, % Used and Temperature Added.

Cure Time.

Notes:

Pass or Fail? _____

Candle Jar Used.

P

Date : _____
Suppliers : _____
Project : _____

Wax and Wick Used.

Costs.

Fragrance Used, % Used, Pour Temperature.

Wax Melt Top Temperature and Pour Temperature.

Dye Used, % Used and Temperature Added.

Cure Time.

Notes:

Pass or Fail ? _____

Candle Jar Used.

P

Date : _____
Suppliers : _____
Project : _____

Wax and Wick Used.

Costs.

Fragrance Used, % Used, Pour Temperature.

Wax Melt Top Temperature and Pour Temperature.

Dye Used, % Used and Temperature Added.

Cure Time.

Notes:

Pass or Fail ? _____

Candle Jar Used.

Date: _____
Suppliers: _____
Project: _____

Wax and Wick Used.

Costs.

Fragrance Used, % Used, Pour Temperature.

Wax Melt Top Temperature and Pour Temperature.

Dye Used, % Used and Temperature Added.

Cure Time.

Notes:

Pass or Fail? _____

Candle Jar Used.

P

Date:
Suppliers:
Project:

Wax and Wick Used.

Costs.

Fragrance Used, % Used, Pour Temperature.

Wax Melt Top Temperature and Pour Temperature.

Dye Used, % Used and Temperature Added.

Cure Time.

Notes:

Pass or Fail?

Candle Jar Used.

Q

Date : _____
Suppliers : _____
Project : _____

Wax and Wick Used.

Costs.

Fragrance Used. % Used. Pour Temperature.

Wax Melt Top Temperature and Pour Temperature.

Dye Used. % Used and Temperature Added.

Cure Time.

Notes:

Pass or Fail ? _____

Candle Jar Used.

Q

Date: _____

Suppliers: _____

Project: _____

Wax and Wick Used.

Costs.

Fragrance Used, % Used, Pour Temperature.

Wax Melt Top Temperature and Pour Temperature.

Dye Used, % Used and Temperature Added.

Cure Time.

Notes:

Pass or Fail? _____

Candle Jar Used.

Date: _____
Suppliers: _____
Project: _____

Wax and Wick Used.

Costs.

Fragrance Used.
% Used. Pour Temperature.

Wax Melt Top Temperature and Pour Temperature.

Dye Used.
% Used and Temperature Added.

Cure Time.

Notes:

Pass or Fail? _____

Candle Jar Used.

Q

Date: _____
Suppliers: _____
Project: _____

Wax and Wick Used.

Costs.

Fragrance Used, % Used, Pour Temperature.

Wax Melt Top Temperature and Pour Temperature. _____

Dye Used, % Used and Temperature Added.

Cure Time.

Notes:

Pass or Fail? _____

Candle Jar Used.

Date: ....
Suppliers: ....
Project: ....

Wax and Wick Used.

Costs.

Fragrance Used, % Used, Pour Temperature.

Wax Melt Top Temperature and Pour Temperature.

Dye Used, % Used and Temperature Added.

Cure Time.

Notes.

Pass or Fail? ....

Candle Jar Used.

Date: _____
Suppliers: _____
Project: _____

Wax and Wick Used.

Costs.

Fragrance Used, % Used, Pour Temperature.

Wax Melt Top Temperature and Pour Temperature.

Dye Used, % Used and Temperature Added.

Cure Time.

Notes:

Pass or Fail? _____

Candle Jar Used.

R

Date: _____
Suppliers: _____
Project: _____

Wax and Wick Used.

Costs.

Fragrance Used, % Used, Pour Temperature.

Wax Melt Top Temperature and Pour Temperature.

Dye Used, % Used and Temperature Added.

Cure Time.

Notes:

Pass or Fail? _____

Candle Jar Used.

R

Date : _____
Suppliers : _____
Project : _____

Wax and Wick Used.

Costs.

Fragrance Used, % Used. Pour Temperature.

Wax Melt Top Temperature and Pour Temperature.

Dye Used, % Used and Temperature Added.

Cure Time.

Notes:

Pass or Fail ? _____

Candle Jar Used.

S

Date: ....
Suppliers: ....
Project: ....

Wax and Wick Used.

Costs.

Fragrance Used, % Used, Pour Temperature.

Wax Melt Top Temperature and Pour Temperature.

Dye Used, % Used and Temperature Added.

Cure Time.

Notes:

Pass or Fail? _____

Candle Jar Used.

S

Date : _____
Suppliers : _____
Project : _____

Wax and Wick Used.

Costs.

Fragrance Used, % Used, Pour Temperature.

Wax Melt Top Temperature and Pour Temperature.

Dye Used, % Used and Temperature Added.

Cure Time.

Notes:

Pass or Fail ? _____

Candle Jar Used.

S

Date: _____

Suppliers: _____

Project: _____

Wax and Wick Used.

Costs.

Fragrance Used, % Used, Pour Temperature.

Wax Melt Top Temperature and Pour Temperature.

Dye Used, % Used and Temperature Added.

Cure Time.

Notes:

Pass or Fail? _____

Candle Jar Used.

Date : _____
Suppliers : _____
Project : _____

Wax and Wick Used.

Costs.

Fragrance Used, % Used, Pour Temperature.

Wax Melt Top Temperature and Pour Temperature.

Dye Used, % Used and Temperature Added.

Cure Time.

Notes:

Pass or Fail ? _____

Candle Jar Used.

T

Date : _____
Suppliers : _____
Project : _____

Wax and Wick Used.

Costs.

Fragrance Used, % Used, Pour Temperature.

Wax Melt Top Temperature and Pour Temperature.

Dye Used, % Used and Temperature Added.

Cure Time.

Notes:

Pass or Fail ? _____

Candle Jar Used.

T

Date: _____
Suppliers: _____
Project: _____

Wax and Wick Used.

Costs.

Fragrance Used, % Used, Pour Temperature.

Wax Melt Top Temperature and Pour Temperature.

Dye Used, % Used and Temperature Added.

Cure Time.

Notes:

Pass or Fail? _____

Candle Jar Used.

T

Date : _____
Suppliers : _____
Project : _____

Wax and Wick Used.

Costs.

Fragrance Used, % Used. Pour Temperature.

Wax Melt Top Temperature and Pour Temperature.

Dye Used, % Used and Temperature Added.

Cure Time.

Notes:

Pass or Fail ? _____

Candle Jar Used.

T

Date : _____
Suppliers : _____
Project : _____

Wax and Wick Used.

Costs.

Fragrance Used, % Used, Pour Temperature.

Wax Melt Top Temperature and Pour Temperature.

Dye Used, % Used and Temperature Added.

Cure Time.

Notes:

Pass or Fail ? _____

Candle Jar Used.

U

Date: _____
Suppliers: _____
Project: _____

Wax and Wick Used.

Costs.

Fragrance Used, % Used, Pour Temperature.

Wax Melt Top Temperature and Pour Temperature.

Dye Used, % Used and Temperature Added.

Cure Time.

Notes:

Pass or Fail? _____

Candle Jar Used.

U

Date: _____
Suppliers: _____
Project: _____

Wax and Wick Used.

Costs.

Fragrance Used, % Used, Pour Temperature.

Wax Melt Top Temperature and Pour Temperature.

Dye Used, % Used and Temperature Added.

Cure Time.

Notes:

Pass or Fail? _____

Candle Jar Used.

U

Date : _____
Suppliers : _____
Project : _____

Wax and Wick Used.

Costs.

Fragrance Used, % Used, Pour Temperature.

Wax Melt Top Temperature and Pour Temperature.

Dye Used, % Used and Temperature Added.

Cure Time.

Notes:

Pass or Fail ? _____

Candle Jar Used.

u

Date : _____
Suppliers : _____
Project : _____

Wax and Wick Used.

Costs.

Fragrance Used, % Used, Pour Temperature.

Wax Melt Top Temperature and Pour Temperature.

Dye Used, % Used and Temperature Added.

Cure Time.

Notes:

Pass or Fail ? _____

Candle Jar Used.

Date: _____
Suppliers: _____
Project: _____

Wax and Wick Used.

Costs.

Fragrance Used, % Used, Pour Temperature.

Wax Melt Top Temperature and Pour Temperature.

Dye Used, % Used and Temperature Added.

Cure Time.

Notes:

Pass or Fail? _____

Candle Jar Used.

Date: _____
Suppliers: _____
Project: _____

Wax and Wick Used.

Costs.

Fragrance Used, % Used, Pour Temperature.

Wax Melt Top Temperature and Pour Temperature.

Dye Used, % Used and Temperature Added.

Cure Time.

Notes:

Pass or Fail? _____

Candle Jar Used.

Date: _____
Suppliers: _____
Project: _____

Wax and Wick Used.

Costs.

Fragrance Used, % Used. Pour Temperature.

Wax Melt Top Temperature and Pour Temperature.

Dye Used, % Used and Temperature Added.

Cure Time.

Notes:

Pass or Fail? _____

Candle Jar Used.

Date: _____
Suppliers: _____
Project: _____

Wax and Wick Used.

Costs.

Fragrance Used, % Used, Pour Temperature.

Wax Melt Top Temperature and Pour Temperature.

Dye Used, % Used and Temperature Added.

Cure Time.

Notes:

Pass or Fail? _____

Candle Jar Used.

W

Date :

Suppliers :

Project :

Wax and Wick Used.

Costs.

Fragrance Used, % Used, Pour Temperature.

Wax Melt Top Temperature and Pour Temperature.

Dye Used, % Used and Temperature Added.

Cure Time.

Notes:

Pass or Fail ?

Candle Jar Used.

W

Date: _____
Suppliers: _____
Project: _____

Wax and Wick Used.

Costs.

Fragrance Used. % Used. Pour Temperature.

Wax Melt Top Temperature and Pour Temperature. _____

Dye Used. % Used and Temperature Added.

Cure Time.

Notes:

Pass or Fail? _____

Candle Jar Used.

W

Date: _____
Suppliers: _____
Project: _____

Wax and Wick Used.

Costs.

Fragrance Used, % Used, Pour Temperature.

Wax Melt Top Temperature and Pour Temperature.

Dye Used, % Used and Temperature Added.

Cure Time.

Notes:

Pass or Fail? _____

Candle Jar Used.

W

Date: _____
Suppliers: _____
Project: _____

Wax and Wick Used.

Costs.

Fragrance Used, % Used, Pour Temperature.

Wax Melt Top Temperature and Pour Temperature.

Dye Used, % Used and Temperature Added.

Cure Time.

Notes:

Pass or Fail? _____

Candle Jar Used.

α

Date : _____
Suppliers : _____
Project : _____

Wax and Wick Used.

Costs.

Fragrance Used, % Used, Pour Temperature.

Wax Melt Top Temperature and Pour Temperature.

Dye Used, % Used and Temperature Added.

Cure Time.

Notes:

Pass or Fail ? _____

Candle Jar Used.

α

Date: _____
Suppliers: _____
Project: _____

Wax and Wick Used.

Costs.

Fragrance Used, % Used, Pour Temperature.

Wax Melt Top Temperature and Pour Temperature.

Dye Used, % Used and Temperature Added.

Cure Time.

Notes:

Pass or Fail? _____

Candle Jar Used.

α

Date : _____
Suppliers : _____
Project : _____

Wax and Wick Used.

Costs.

Fragrance Used, % Used, Pour Temperature.

Wax Melt Top Temperature and Pour Temperature.

Dye Used, % Used and Temperature Added.

Cure Time.

Notes:

Pass or Fail ? _____

Candle Jar Used.

α

Date : _____

Suppliers : _____

Project : _____

Wax and Wick Used.

Costs.

Fragrance Used, % Used, Pour Temperature.

Wax Melt Top Temperature and Pour Temperature.

_____

Dye Used, % Used and Temperature Added.

Cure Time.

Notes:

Pass or Fail ? _____

Candle Jar Used.

y

Date : _____

Suppliers : _____

Project : _____

Wax and Wick Used.

Costs.

Fragrance Used, % Used, Pour Temperature.

Wax Melt Top Temperature and Pour Temperature.

Dye Used, % Used and Temperature Added.

Cure Time.

Notes:

Pass or Fail ? _____

Candle Jar Used.

y

Date : _____
Suppliers : _____
Project : _____

Wax and Wick Used.

Costs.

Fragrance Used, % Used, Pour Temperature.

Wax Melt Top Temperature and Pour Temperature.

Dye Used, % Used and Temperature Added.

Cure Time.

Notes:

Pass or Fail ? _____

Candle Jar Used.

Date: _____
Suppliers: _____
Project: _____

Wax and Wick Used.

Costs.

Fragrance Used, % Used, Pour Temperature.

Wax Melt Top Temperature and Pour Temperature.

Dye Used, % Used and Temperature Added.

Cure Time.

Notes:

Pass or Fail? _____

Candle Jar Used.

Date: _____
Suppliers: _____
Project: _____

Wax and Wick Used.

Costs.

Fragrance Used, % Used. Pour Temperature.

Wax Melt Top Temperature and Pour Temperature. _____

Dye Used, % Used and Temperature Added.

Cure Time.

Notes:

Pass or Fail? _____

Candle Jar Used.

3

Date: _____
Suppliers: _____
Project: _____

Wax and Wick Used.

Costs.

Fragrance Used, % Used, Pour Temperature.

Wax Melt Top Temperature and Pour Temperature.

Dye Used, % Used and Temperature Added.

Cure Time.

Notes:

Pass or Fail? _____

Candle Jar Used.

3

Date: _____
Suppliers: _____
Project: _____

Wax and Wick Used.

Costs.

Fragrance Used, % Used, Pour Temperature.

Wax Melt Top Temperature and Pour Temperature.

Dye Used, % Used and Temperature Added.

Cure Time.

Notes:

Pass or Fail? _____

Candle Jar Used.

3

Date: _____
Suppliers: _____
Project: _____

Wax and Wick Used.

Costs.

Fragrance Used. % Used. Pour Temperature.

Wax Melt Top Temperature and Pour Temperature. _____

Dye Used. % Used and Temperature Added.

Cure Time.

Notes:

Pass or Fail ? _____

Candle Jar Used.

3

Date: _____
Suppliers: _____
Project: _____

Wax and Wick Used.

Costs.

Fragrance Used, % Used, Pour Temperature.

Wax Melt Top Temperature and Pour Temperature.

Dye Used, % Used and Temperature Added.

Cure Time.

Notes:

Pass or Fail? _____

Candle Jar Used.

Notes.

Notes.

Notes.

Notes.

Notes.

Notes.

Notes.

Notes.

Notes.

Notes.

Notes.

Notes.

Notes.

Notes.

www.ingramcontent.com/pod-product-compliance
Lightning Source LLC
LaVergne TN
LVHW011957070526
838202LV00054B/4950